About Me

My name is David. I am a survivor.
I have survived various "character-building" events such as living rough on the streets of England, being lost at sea in a canoe, being stranded in the mountains during winter, being attacked with knives and bats, and having to defend my living space from armed invasion.

I have had to catch, scavenge or steal food, live with the pain of broken bones when there was no medical attention available, and above all, I have had to develop the right mental toughness that is possibly the most important factor in survival.
I have had to put into practice the very things which you will find in this book - the things which will keep you and your loved ones alive when the shit hits the fan.

Although I have not had military experience, I have had extensive experience of being on my own, with no support and no supplies, starving, and sometimes with injuries and with people trying to harm me. I believe that what I learnt during those few dark years has uniquely prepared me for the future - a future without government help, where the emergency services no longer exist, and where your neighbours arm themselves to take your food.

My experiences were gained over a period of several years in the 1990's, and thankfully I now have a good job and a loving family. But like most of you, I am concerned with the way the world is going, and I want to be absolutely sure I can keep my family safe. I feel that as a man, a husband and a father, it is my duty to protect my family no matter how much shit hits the fan, and like you, I will do whatever I have to to keep them safe.

Introduction

This is not so much a "how to" book as a call to action, and it contains practical advice that has been put to the test in the real world under conditions of starvation and attack.

I will not be suggesting that at the end of the world humanity will pull together and we'll all be walking around holding hands and sharing food. I'm afraid the reality of survival, particularly when everything is lost, is that there'll be times when you'll have to fight for your life.

We will be having an honest, no nonsense look at personal survival when you and your family are absolutely on your own, cut off, without help, starving and under attack. We'll look at all the things you'll need to prepare for, and hopefully by the end of the book you'll understand that you confrontation is one of the things you need to be training for.
We'll be looking at survival from the worst possible case scenario, where you'll be surviving long term without government help after the total breakdown of society. This will be back to basics living, a caveman existence where your only preoccupations will be food and water, fighting, and shelter.

I will not be telling you to spend a fortune on generators, on several tons of food etc. I will instead be telling you that in a world where gangs and neighbours want to take your life and your supplies, your greatest asset could be your ability to be inconspicuous. You should be hiding and thriving, not advertising your booty. You should be able to be mobile and able to react to any situation, remembering that although we can plan and prepare, the nature of survival is very fluid.

Also, I'm encouraging you to remember that it is possible to live on a lot less than you might imagine. At one point in my life all I had were my clothes, a tin opener, and an empty dustbin bag. Of course I was aware of how little I had, but I didn't starve and I am here to tell the tale today.

That's an important message for those of us who are planning to survive the future. You don't need to spend a fortune on your gear, and more importantly, you might not actually have a fortune to spend. It is too easy to look at all the kit on the market and to get disheartened because it is too expensive, but the reality is that a lot of it is superfluous either because it is not actually of any use in a real survival situation, or because there are cheaper and better alternatives.

For example, there are military style digital watches available to us - super tough and designed to last - but an EMP attack would render them useless. I know a chap who spent £1499 on his watch, which is outrageous.

An analogue watch is better because you can use it as a compass, and if the watch is kinetic then you won't need to carry around a stock of batteries.

It is too easy to become seduced by gear and to rely too heavily on it. By far the best thing you can do with your money is to use it to get training in vital skills such as bushcraft, wild food, martial arts, first aid etc. At a push, you could make do with whatever equipment you have lying around the house, but you can't make do with limited knowledge. Knowledge is survival.

We'll have a proper look at kit later on in the book...

My own personal experience shows that in a total survival situation perhaps the greatest threat is from your fellow survivors.

I am a humanist, but I am also a realist. If you have food, water, and the means to defend yourself and your family, then other survivors will want to take those things off you. That's not a judgement, it's a fact. Perhaps they're just doing what you'll be doing yourself if your own food runs out.

Your priority, your only reason for living, is to protect and feed your family isn't it? These other survivors feel the same and they'll need to get supplies at all costs, even if it means killing you for it.

The sad truth is that eventually if the survival situation continues for any length of time, there will also be individuals and gangs who kill or rape for sport rather than just survival. This is what you have to be prepared for.

Of course, there will be groups of people who band together to protect each other and to share resources, and that's fantastic. That's the best we can hope for at the end. But there will be times when you'll be entirely on your own and you'll have to rely on your own skills and ingenuity to keep your family alive.

This pattern of aggressive behaviour in total survival situations is validated by several reports from overseas disasters. Remember, we're talking about the total disintegration of society here. The absolute destruction of everything we know. No law and order, no healthcare, no protection, no future. There are so many different ways this could happen, from supervolcano, asteroid, nuclear war, EMP attack etc. I have seen fights over food and they are not pretty, and I remember punch ups when there were fuel shortages a few years ago. Imagine these situations when life depends on each combatant getting hold of whatever they are fighting over. Imagine what it will be like when everyone knows that they are going to die if they don't get their hands on food.

In these circumstances humans change. We become feral, and all the societal barriers to aggression come tumbling down. The first reaction to any major disaster is often shock and disbelief. It is followed by panic of varying levels, and then violence, chaos, and total breakdown.
Society always seems to build itself up again over time, although not necessarily in the same form as before.
During Hurricane Katrina for example, people were killed for food and property. Reports say there were gangs of criminals raping and killing people, gangs of vigilantes killing other gangs, and no law and order to protect anyone.
After the worst of the chaos had died down, gangs controlled different areas of New Orleans, imposing a kind of martial law.

This dramatic reaction by the residents of New Orleans came about because they thought their world had ended. The force of nature was so strong that their immediate world was destroyed, and with no sign of authority or government, they took the law and their futures into their own hands.

The point we need to bear in mind is that the total breakdown of law and order started more or less immediately, with unchecked violence and shops and houses being stripped of food and property.
Of course I accept that New Orleans is different to Harrogate, for example! Maybe it would take a while longer for the residents of Harrogate to behave in the same way, but I've seen it happen in my own life on a much smaller scale. People always seem to come together and behave as a pack. Every leafy, middle-class town in England will have packs of feral aggressors when the world ends...

Ready To Survive

I am no psychologist, but I've often wondered if people could be divided into two distinct camps - reactive personalities, and proactive personalities.
The reactive type doesn't plan or prepare. The shops are all locked up because we're in the grip of a worldwide pandemic, but the reactive type thinks to himself that he will stroll down and buy a few extra tins of corned beef when the shops reopen.

The proactive type thinks to himself - "Am I prepared? Have I secured the house, got enough food and water, medicine, weapons? What about my bugout bag, my exit plan, my rally point in case my family get separated? Have I learnt what wild food is edible? Does everyone in my group know what their individual responsibilities are? Have I taken care of myself - improved my fitness, gone to martial art classes? Have I got a plan for long term survival?"

Perhaps the most important question to be asked, is "Am I mentally prepared for this?" What if to feed your family you had to break into a shop to steal food? Or arm yourself and go out to fight an armed survivor for it? Or grab your machete and fight off the neighbours who are breaking into your house to steal your food?
Survival - real, back against the wall survival - is not pretty.

Before you start to think about weapons and supplies, there are three key things that you need to get in your mind before you can be a survivor.

They are -

Mentality
This is the "X-Factor" of the survival world. It's something you either have or you don't, although it can be cultivated and learnt.
You need to have the mentality of a survivor. You must WANT to survive, and perhaps, you must ENJOY this new world.
A survivor thrives on the challenges of finding food for himself and his family. He loves learning the skills that prepare him for any catastrophe, such as first aid or martial arts. He relishes pushing himself to beat previous bests in his fitness routines. He is not a psychopath, but he is honourable enough to be prepared to arm himself and go outside to protect a stranger from a rapist.
Beyond courage, a survivor mentality is one of self reliance. A survivor doesn't moan and complain when the government no longer feeds him and he must fend for himself. A survivor is prepared to raid shops if necessary to feed his family. He has a mentality of a leader - a decision maker - one who directs his own survival and that of his family, rather than waiting to be rescued or butchered.

Training
Physical and mental fitness is perhaps the most important requirement of a survivor, and both your body and your mind can be trained and improved.

You must be physically fit and strong, and trained in at least one martial art. You should be an expert in your chosen weapons. Fitness training should be part of your every day pre-apocalypse life. Once the shit hits the fan you will effectively be living as a soldier behind enemy lines, so you should expect to need the same fitness levels as a soldier. Mental fitness is vital so that you don't crack under the pressure or give up, particularly if you lose loved ones. Another benefit of mental fitness is that you don't become a psychopath. You are able to retain your sense of empathy toward your fellow survivors, and you work to build up society rather than take advantage of its downfall.
I remember a phrase someone told me once - "Don't give a sword to a man who can't dance."
This was apparently something ancient Britons believed, that if a man couldn't see beauty in things then he shouldn't be given a sword. A psychopath is someone who fights for no reason, whereas a healthy person is one who fights only to protect.
Training also includes your chosen equipment. If you have walkie-talkies, do you know how to change channels? Can you work your camping stove, and do you know how to use a flint and steel?
A quick word on martial arts - many of us blokes are a bit over-confident, and we think we'll be alright in a fight. Maybe you had a few Karate lessons twenty years ago and you think that's enough to see you through a fight.
The reality of a fight is often very different to what we imagine in our minds. Under the stress of a violent encounter you slow down, you become inaccurate, and your punches lack power. The person who is attacking you is feeling a rush of adrenaline or rage, and he can't actually feel your punches.
I can't stress enough the importance of up to date martial arts training, particularly in a style that teaches you how to end a fight quickly. There are no rules when you are fighting for your life - you must be trained and prepared to do whatever violence you need to to survive.

Awareness
In a survival situation there is a time for reactive actions, and a time for proactive actions. We need to be proactively aware of our situation, which means we keep watch, we listen, we talk to other survivors. This in turn means we can react accordingly.
Knowledge of your surroundings is vital. You must be aware of all your local escape routes, places you can hide up, places that are easily defensible and those that are not.
You must keep your eyes and ears open, watching and listening for movement.
A small pair of binoculars take up very little room but are useful for guarding the road outside your house or looking for movement within other houses. If you're in transit, they're great for scanning the route ahead to look for ambushes.
As you travel you must be constantly aware and vigilant. Aware of wild food opportunities, vigilant against dangers.

Being Prepared

A well-prepared person has options, a victim has none.

I'll say this several times throughout the book - your goal in surviving should be to maintain a secure primary defensible position - a home.
In the context of "preparedness" there is often too great an emphasis on "bugging out", and I imagine that's because we've more or less inherited the idea of "prepping" from our American cousins. I can completely understand the concept from the point of view of an American. With their vast wildernesses it makes perfect sense to leave overpopulated cities where everyone has a gun, and take your chances in nature.
From our British point of view it makes little sense, and certainly from a defensive perspective it may be foolhardy.

Although a crowbar and fire will allow access to almost any home, it is possible to take steps to slow down intruders so that you can effectively defend your home from invasion. Chicken wire tacked over the windows, doors glued and nailed shut, nails pointing upwards through the carpets etc. All these will slow attackers down and allow you to either escape or defend. Defence should be your first choice unless you are facing insurmountable odds, but even if there are hordes of aggressors in your home you can still fight effectively even if you are on your own.

A narrow hallway or staircase is perfect for hacking or stabbing with a sword, garden fork or homemade spear. These choke points should be narrowed further with strategically placed bookcases, wardrobes or any other obstacle you can find that means only one person can get through at a time.

Remember, in a melee such as this you are just hacking and slashing, using ultra-violence rather than skillful and artistic fencing skills. This sort of defence is only possible if your aggressors don't have projectile weapons such as guns or bows. If they are armed like that then you'd best get out in plenty of time.

The most effective way to defeat an attacker is through speed, surprise and aggression. Assuming we're waiting to be attacked, and therefore we don't have the advantage of surprise, that leaves speed and aggression.

Speed means that we don't spar. We don't stand-off and trade punches, we get stuck in and end a fight quickly using the next skill - aggression. We must be violent and merciless, especially if there are multiple attackers and your life and the lives of your family are at stake.

Once intruders have got inside your house, you'll have to do whatever the situation and your conscience allows.

If society had utterly collapsed and these people were breaking in to steal your food and rape your wife, you'd do whatever it took, wouldn't you?

What will we need to store at home?

I know a chap who has over a ton of long life food stored in two spare rooms in his house. Personally I don't think it's a good idea, but I know that there are plenty of other people who do the same.

My own thoughts are that if you're going to store that much food then it should be locked away and concealed, rather than just dumped in two rooms where fire and intruders can get to it.

I know that home defence is our priority, but I am not optimistic enough to think I'd be able to single handedly fight off an armed gang of fifty starving yobs. Maybe I won't be alone. Maybe I'll have joined a collaboration of neighbours to keep us all safe, but I would have thought my stockpile of food would have to be used as currency. I'd surely have to share it around to keep everyone motivated in defending our street. Ideally, and I know it sounds heartless, my stockpile will be used to feed my family, and I won't be sharing it. Family first. I've been in this situation before when I was homeless for a while, and I know that although you can be all altruistic and think you'd be the one sharing your food with others, when the time actually comes and you are starving for real, you'll be prepared to fight for that food with your life. And if there's someone you love starving next to you, you'll give them the food and protect their right to eat it with your life.

Anyway, back to the subject. A ton of food cannot be easily hidden. You could put it in the attic on the basis that looters will look for food in the kitchen and then ransack the rest of the house, but they usually (but not always) ignore the attic.

Your best best is to dig some sort of cellar under your garden and bury it all, after making sure you'd packed it away in air tight, moisture proof containers.

But even then you'd need a huge hole, and you might not have the time to dig it.

That always seems like a strange truth to me, that we consider ourselves prepared yet we can make excuses for why we're actually not totally prepared.

Take home security for example. I could go around installing steel shutters on my doors and windows, but I can't afford it, my wife wouldn't let me, and we might be moving house soon anyway.
What about the huge hole in the garden for the ton of survival foods?
Such a hole is massive and again, my wife would object. We only have a small garden and it would basically mean digging it all up.
My point is that it is all very well trying to be prepared, but there are limitations to how far most of us can realistically go. Lack of money, lack of time, lack of space, unwilling spouses. All these things can hinder us but they're actually good training for the future, when we must always be able to react to the fluidity of survival situations. These obstacles give us the opportunity to use our ingenuity to come up with alternative solutions.

Take the lack of steel shutters as an example. It won't provide as much of a defensive capability, but you could use chicken wire instead. Chicken wire tacked to the internal brickwork surrounding your windows means that anyone who smashed the glass to get in would not be able to quickly get past the wire. Access through doors can be hindered by glueing and bolting the door to the frame, progress can be impeded by nails poking up through the carpet and by using furniture to create choke points on narrow hallways. Barricades can be built by piling up tables, chairs, chest of drawers etc.

And is there really any alternative to having a ton of food stored up?
You could buy a bit at a time. So on your weekly shop you can add a couple of tins for your survival stash until you've built up a supply that you're happy with.
But how long will that take? What if the end of the world happens tonight? That won't leave you with many options. I'm not rich enough to be able to buy a year's survival food and we only have a tiny house, so here's what I've done...

I have enough survival food to last myself, my wife and my two young children for three months. This is in addition to the food in our larder for every day use. Our larder is always full up. The three months' food is to be rationed and supplemented with other food which I will be scavenging for. I have spent many years learning what wild food can be eaten from the woods and countryside around our house, and even in winter I am able to eat reasonably well off the land. **You need to be learning about wild food as your main priority.**

By my calculations, by supplementing the rations with the wild food we will have plenty to live off for a year. After that point we will be more reliant on found food, wild food and growing crops. Nature provides a surprisingly abundant wild harvest from the land around us, and I am confident that providing the land isn't contaminated by something (eg nuclear fallout), we'll be able to go on indefinitely.
Just in case the land is contaminated by fallout, I have already dug a very deep hole, deep enough to protect the contents from the fallout, and hidden sacks of compost, some survival rations and some vegetable seed packets.

We also have a well-stocked vegetable garden, although it's fair to say that it's likely to be raided by intruders. And in fact, it's best to always plan for having several vegetable gardens for that very reason. Also if one garden suffers a crop failure for whatever reason, there will be backups.
Our survival food is hidden away in six different locations in the house, under the garden, and in an isolated spot in the woods. I also have plenty of vegetable seed packets so that I can grow food.
Finally, I have plenty of seasoning. Wild food tastes different to what we're used to. Not everyone likes it, and the truth is that some of it tastes downright horrible. Plenty of seasoning helps disguise the taste!
But you don't eat wild food in the same way is "normal" food. Rather than getting a plate of leaves and berries and scoffing the lot, you're much better off nibbling on it throughout the

day. Graze on it. You'll probably make yourself sick if you try to eat it all in one go.

Bear in mind that scavenging for food will become your main (or only) daily routine at the end of the world. Before your supplies have run out you will of course be checking looted shops and empty houses in the hope of resupply.
Also bearing in mind that we're not all rich enough to have enough food bought and stored to feed our families for a significant length of time, you'll also have to make a hard decision on exactly how you are prepared to get food when you realise you're going to run out. For example, do you loot shops once the shit hits the fan? Everyone else will be. If you wait until you're running out, there won't be any left for you to loot.
Is it OK to break the law, just because everyone else will be?

If you haven't got enough food bought and stored, what are the alternatives to looting? Would you rely on growing crops? Have you planned for crop failures, theft, the fact that it can take months to get anything edible from them? Have you read up on how and when to grow vegetables and how to preserve them?
How else could you get food? There's wild food of course - are you knowledgeable enough to be able to live off the land, and does your location provide enough wild food?
How about taking food off other survivors? I have read that during a recent time of famine in North Korea, the people who survived were the ones who took food off others. If it's a matter of life and death would you do it?

I live in a small village. There is only one supermarket within a ten mile radius, so it is always packed and there is often nowhere to park. It has armoured windows and anti-vehicle steel posts every six feet along the outside. In other words, it would be impossible to ram raid.
Upon the realisation that food supplies were going to run out, thousands of people would all descend on this one supermarket. The roads would be blocked and would remain

that way, people would be trampled to death or murdered, and within minutes the entire stock will have been taken.
In a town or city you're likely to have the same problem, so a better plan is to recce your local area and identify the smaller outlets which are easier to access. You'll have to decide very early on if this is a course of action you can justify. Also think about the hard working shopkeeper who may not yet understand how serious the survival situation has become. What if you break in and he lives in a flat above the shop, and he comes down to rightfully defend his property. What happens then?

While you are out looking at the more vulnerable food outlets, make sure you find out where the local allotments are so you can take some crops.

For water, we're well equipped with water filters and we've got a good amount of bottled water hidden away. I was able to bulk-purchase some 15lt water cooler bottles, which means we'll have plenty to keep us going once the mains is turned off.
As well as that we'd plan to fill every spare container once the shit hits the fan, and there's a stream in the woods that we'd be able to get "wild water" from (assuming there's no contamination).

On top of the food and water which you'll have to hide, other things to consider when you're thinking about where to stash your supplies include weapons, first aid kit, fire fighting equipment, bug out bags, clothes.
These are all things which need to be readily available yet as concealed as possible, if only to protect them from a casual burglar who might get in while you're at work.
It would be sod's law if your hard work was destroyed not by an armed gang of survivors, but by some opportunist scumbag.

For practicalities, I've dug a compost toilet in the garden. We haven't tested it yet, but there's nothing to test really. It's just a four foot deep hole, and when you've shat you put some soil over the poo.

Other practicalities include lighting. For the most part we'll want to be invisible, but we have the option of using 8 hour tealights for light. Obviously we've got several torches as well, but we'd rather save them for emergencies. We don't fancy blundering through the woods in the dark if we have to bug out in a hurry.

For cooking we have several options. We have a firepit in the garden, although of course we'd be remarkably daft to allow the aroma of cooking food to spread through the area. Remember, people are starving and are prepared to kill you for your food.
We have a camping stove and several bottles of gas, and we have a couple of tiny solid fuel stoves which we're saving for our bug out. Finally, my wife and I can start a fire from found materials.
However the reality of survival food is that most of it can be eaten cold and uncooked. Wild meat needs to be cooked obviously, and freshwater fish.

Boredom is another thing to consider, and although we who like to be prepared can be kept entertained for hours by checking and rechecking our supplies or by cleaning weapons, younger family members and those who are addicted to the television are not so easily amused.
Remember that you are trying to be inconspicuous, and don't let people play on their tablets without making sure they understand that they could endanger lives. There's unlikely to be any internet, but if people are watching downloaded films, listening to music or playing games, they're going to advertise your presence.
A wind-up radio could be a vital source of information and it should be an essential part of your kit, but listen to it with the volume low or with headphones.
Of course, if the end is caused by a massive EMP then none of these gadgets will work anyway.

Boredom can be a killer because people can become disobedient, distracted, half asleep and generally ineffective. Survival requires you to be "switched on" at all times, and when you allow yourself to "switch off" for a few hours sleep, you need to know that there's someone keeping watch who can be totally relied upon. A sulky teenager who is huffing and puffing because they've got withdrawal symptoms from not being able to watch crap on TV, is going to get you all killed. Playing "I Spy" probably won't work. Nor will your stock of board games.

If the times are still tense then most people will be occupied with keeping an eye out for the next threat, or they'll be wired from all the drama and won't have thought about the telly. But during down times they'll realise how bored they are.

You have to keep the members of your family occupied by giving them tasks. Hopefully you'll have a collection of useful books that you'll have bought and studied as part of your preparation plans - first aid, bushcraft, vegetable growing etc? Why not make each person responsible for thoroughly learning a particular subject and then teaching the other members of your group?

As well as alleviating the boredom, the sense of responsibility should instill a feeling of value in whoever you've given the task to. A sense of pride maybe. All this helps with morale.

Essentially, this is your checklist for creating a place in which to live out the end of the world -

- Is it secure?
- Can you conceal plenty of survival rations (food and water)?
- Is it near an area where you can readily source wild food?
- Are you able to grow vegetables?
- Can you make an outside loo?
- Have you made several escape plans and made everyone aware of them?

There are a few things you should make sure you have at home in addition to your food, water, and general daily living supplies. Here's what I consider to be essential, but you'll notice how short the list is! Feel free to add or take away whatever you personally prefer.

First Aid Kit
Antiseptic
Tweezers
Latex Free Gloves
Dust Masks
Goggles
Soap
Disinfectant
Wind Up Radio
Wind Up Torch
Spare Batteries
Torches
Fire Fighting Equipment
DIY Tools including nails, bolts etc
MDF or Planks for Repairs
Chicken Wire

Staying Put or Bugging Out

Your goal should always be to have a solid, defensible position. Bugging out is the term we use for relocating, rather than necessarily for permanent wilderness living.
Your bugging out bag will contain some essentials that will keep you alive while you relocate, but the contents are not intended for long term survival. If you tried to fit absolutely everything you needed for long term survival in a rucksack, it would be too heavy to carry.

Staying put involves the decision to prepare and fortify your supplies and your home. Only you will know whether that's the best course of action, and that decision will be based on local factors such as risk of home invasion, escalation of disaster, risk of contamination etc. But you'll also need to consider HOW you would bug out, and whether leaving your home would put you in greater danger than staying put.

For example, would you go in a vehicle or on foot? Roads will get blocked by other traffic. If you're on foot you could be attacked or separated from your family. Either way you run the risk of becoming a homeless refugee.
If you are staying put you will need to secure your supplies. This means hiding them, locking them away, and having a plan in place to retrieve them if your house gets taken over.

It's a hard choice whether or not to leave your home. As I say, it depends on so many variables that only you will be able to make a decision on, but the main factor has to be - "What will keep my family safe?"
There could be situations of mass panic and violence, where simply stepping outside your house could get you killed.

Remember, we're not talking about a minor inconvenience such as a power cut, we're talking about end of the world style disaster, massive loss of life, a complete breakdown of society.

Where would you go if you left your house?
Bearing in mind the potential dangers of traveling through what has become hostile territory, you must have a plan and a backup plan, and then a couple more backups too. Make sure everyone in your group understands each of them.

Would you -

- Head to your workplace. It is easy enough to defend and as it's an office nobody will think of breaking in to look for food.
- Go to the police station or local barracks. You'll be safe there as they have loads of guns.
- Head to the hospital, another safe place.
- Go to a friend or relative's house.
- Invade a stranger's house and turf them out.

First off, you can forget about hospitals, police stations and barracks. They'll either be packed with panicky people or closed to refugees (you). If a barrack is open to refugees it is likely that your freedom of movement will be restricted, so you can't leave easily.

Anyway, it's not unusual in total disasters for military personnel to desert their posts and go home to look after their families.

A friend or a relative could put you up, and if you can pool resources and fight as a team you'll all be more effective. If you have a local friend who is as prepared as you are, and you've agreed a plan beforehand, you're very lucky!

Your workplace might be a good idea, although of course, only you will know whether or not it is defensible.

What about finding a good, strong looking house where your family will be safe, and turfing out whoever lives there? Family comes first, surely?

You have to imagine that if the shit had well and truly hit the fan and you were sitting in your house and the doorbell rang, you probably wouldn't answer it if you didn't recognise the people at your door. So you'd have to try and break in and hope whoever was inside wasn't armed. Maybe the house has ten ex SAS blokes inside.

This is where proactive planning is so important. You must come up with a plan NOW, do your research, recce the area and explain the plan to everyone in your group, so that when the time comes you all know exactly what you're doing.

Whether you're bugging out or staying put, it makes sense from a security perspective to NOT put all your food and supplies in one place. Personally, I have my main stash in a locked and hidden location, and then smaller stashes dotted around the house and garden. A stash can be buried, hidden behind plasterboard walls, disguised etc, so that even if you lose one or more sets of supplies, there will be others available to you.

Another option when it comes to food rations and other supplies, is to have several caches dotted around the local area. This would usually mean wrapping everything in plastic, putting it all in tupperware containers and then burying it, so it's only really possible if you live somewhere where you won't be observed.

It is important that you also have some caches near or at your planned bug out location - the place you have decided on relocating to if your primary defensive position (your house) falls.

So let's focus on staying put for now, as that is our primary goal.

The checklist for staying put includes -

1. For long term survival, can I plant a vegetable patch and have an outdoor loo?
2. Are the boundaries secure - can I easily see approaching threats?
3. Is the house secure externally - it is very hard for people to break in?
4. Is the house secure internally - can I channel intruders down a particular path, or deny them access to certain areas?
5. What is my role?
6. Does my family know what each of them must do - firefighter, first aider, fighter, equipment carrier etc?
7. Can I easily communicate with all members of my family in the event of an attack?
8. Does everyone in my family know the escape plan, how to get out of the house if we're over-run, where our rally point is, where our secondary rally point is if the first is unreachable, and where our final and backup destinations are?
9. Are we equipped with fire fighting equipment?
10. Are our supplies safe and can we recover them if the house is taken?

Let's look at a potential scenario in which we have fortified our house as best we can, and prepared an escape plan for when we're over-run -

It is just three days since a worldwide disaster brought society to a standstill. There is no communication, no television or radio signals. The Police are nowhere to be seen and the hospitals are over-run with scared and sick people.
The roads are blocked with abandoned vehicles. There is no fuel, no power, and the shops have been emptied by looters. There has been an escalation in the level of violence as people start to panic. What started as fist fights have become armed encounters.
Garden implements, knives, bats, crossbows and shotguns are used more and more frequently as neighbours turn on each other and fight over food. The streets are packed with panicky people and I can see gangs of people going house to house, breaking in and savagely attacking the people inside before stealing their food.
We live in a terraced house with a shared garden at the front and standard six foot wooden fence panels at the back. I am the only member of my family capable of fighting. My wife will be looking after our two children who are too young to help in any way.

Using the checklist above, I can instantly say that -
1. **For long term survival, can I plant a vegetable patch and have an outdoor loo?**
We have raised beds for growing vegetables, and a compost toilet.

2. **Are the boundaries secure - can I easily see approaching threats?**
The boundaries are secure in that I can see approaching threats front and back, although there are no barriers which are strong enough to stop people getting onto my property.

3. **Is the house secure externally - it is very hard for people to break in?**
The house is reasonably secure externally, although due to the poor construction I have had to bolt planks across the front and back doors, and the downstairs windows. Modern building methods are designed to save money, not to increase

security. A crowbar could force open most windows and doors, and older UPVC front doors bend when you kick them in the middle, making it possible to force the multipoint locks out.

4. **Is the house secure internally - can I channel intruders down a particular path, or deny them access to certain areas?**

I have put bolts and locks on the downstairs internal doors, as well as used Gorilla Glue between the door and the frame. This will slow down intruders rather than stop them entirely. They will ultimately be able to break the doors down, but it will at least hinder the intruders and leave them exposed should I choose to attack them. I have put sharpened nails pointing upwards throughout the carpeted areas, to hurt any intruders wearing trainers. I have already taken a crowbar and removed the stairs so that my family will be safe upstairs. We have a ladder so we can get up and down, and when we're all upstairs we'll pull the ladder up so nobody can follow.

5. **What is my role?**

I will be downstairs defending the house. If it's just a few neighbours I can fight them off on my own, but if it's a large and armed gang, once I'm sure we're getting over-run, I will swallow my pride and climb the ladder to safety. I could use a can of deodorant and a cigarette lighter as an improvised flame thrower aimed at attackers through the window, or maybe a crossbow. However, knowing when NOT to fight is important when you have a vulnerable family to protect.

6. **Does my family know what each of them must do - firefighter, first aider, fighter, equipment carrier etc?**

My wife is a good first aider but my children don't have roles because they are so young.

7. **Can I easily communicate with all members of my family in the event of an attack?**

My wife and I have walkie talkies. We can easily talk to each other in the house, but the talkies are just in case we get separated when we're outside.

8. **Does everyone in my family know the escape plan, how to get out of the house if we're over-run, where our rally point is, where our secondary rally point is if the first is unreachable, and where our final and backup destinations are?**

Our escape plan is this... Once we're all upstairs we will climb into the attic. I will grab our bug out bag and we will then break out onto the roof by smashing through the tiles using the hatchet which we keep up there. As we are in a terraced house we could then crawl across the roofs to the end of the terrace and make our way down via the windows in a loft extension. Or, at any point we could gain access to another house by breaking through their roof tiles. In case we get split up, we all know where our first rally point is - our house backs onto woodland and there's a particular spot we all know. Our secondary rally point is a quarter mile further into the woods, again at a point we all know well. It should be noted that in total urban chaos, all rally points are likely to be compromised. Ideally you'll want a place where your family will be safe if you get separated. That's why I chose our woods, on the basis that people will be more unlikely to be in them. Our agreed final destination is a particular building which is a couple of miles down an overgrown track, and our backup location is two miles beyond that. My wife and I have discussed and agreed at which point each backup location becomes the active one. This is important in case we get separated.

9. **Are we equipped with fire fighting equipment?**
We have fire fighting equipment in case the intruders try to burn us out.

10. **Are our supplies safe and can we recover them if the house is taken?**
Our supplies are safe. They won't be found and I am confident I will be able to recover them if the house is taken.

You can see that this example is an extreme case - one of armed invasion by too many people for me to defend against. In any lesser situation I would stay put and fight intruders off. A bug out, as I keep saying, is a relocation - an emergency evacuation when you believe you're going to die if you stay put. It's a last resort.

Many houses are like mine - built on a budget - and you can only defend them as far as your ability or your budget allows. You could, for example, spend lots of money installing steel shutters on the doors and windows, or building a hidden underground shelter similar to a hurricane shelter.

There are also plenty of houses that are better built than mine - you may be lucky enough to be in one - but with a crowbar and maybe some fire, almost any building can be breached. Of course, there are things you can do to slow people down, such as bolting internal barricades (planks of wood) against doors and windows, and you need to remember to have the right tools and equipment to repair any damage done by intruders, and make your house secure again.

Also, bear in mind that nailing planks of wood across doors and windows will slow attackers down, but it won't stop them indefinitely. You're better off sinking bolts into the brickwork around doors and windows, and then attaching the planks to them using wide washers and nuts.

Fire is one of the reasons why I am not a fan of a "safe room". Assuming your house is of solid construction, maybe you have a basement? But if the rest of the house is on fire you're trapped.

Some people think of an attic as a safe room on the basis that you need a ladder to get into it, only one attacker at a time can go up, and you can easily make the loft hatch secure by putting something heavy on it. But again, fire will kill you.

It is so important to have an escape plan that everyone in your family understands inside and out. It needs to become second nature, so that when an attack comes, everyone knows what is expected of them.

What if you live in a bungalow, how would you defend it? My thoughts are that you either prepare yourself to repel all intruders using whatever means you can, or you leave before it all turns ugly. Any building could be modified to make it defensible if you have time and money, but what if you don't? It doesn't take long for society to collapse into lawlessness following a huge disaster, and there certainly won't be enough time for you to make major alterations to your house once the end is here.

A flat can be defended if you are on anything other than the ground floor, but the weakness is that you are limited in your exit options. There should be a fire escape hopefully, but potential intruders are likely to be using that. The stairs in blocks of flats are often concrete, which means they can't be removed in a hurry as a defensive measure.
Also, in a flat you are less likely to have the option of being able to grow your own food, which is essential for long term survival. Of course you could use troughs if they can get enough light, but you won't be growing a lot of food. Any food is better than no food though.

You need to make an assessment of your home and weigh up the following points -

- Can you defend it in it's current state?
- Can you make alterations to make it defensible, and are you prepared to bearing in mind this might never happen?
- Can you easily and safely get out, particularly if throngs of violent neighbours are outside?

If the answer to any of these questions is "No", then your survival plan should include a thorough look at how you intend to break out and occupy / defend another building, whether that building be your workplace, the home of a friend, or an empty house that you can commandeer.

Any house can only be defended for as long as you are prepared to do so. You need to be aware at all times of your escape route, and act early enough to ensure your family's survival. If you stay and fight too long you could leave your family with no chance of escape, and even if they get out of a burning house without injury, there's the violent mob outside to consider.

I have been in a barricade situation and believe me, it is not pleasant! My best advice is to carefully and quickly look at the odds and determine whether it's worth fighting, be ready to go, and when you go do it quickly.

Sure you are losing your house, but your supplies should be safely stashed and your family will be safe. Hopefully when the invaders don't find your food and weapons, they'll leave and you will be able to return to your house once it's safe.

For long term survival, you'll want to be able to grow some vegetables and have an outside toilet. We have a mixture of raised beds and troughs. The troughs can be moved if necessary. I have also done some "guerilla gardening" and planted vegetables throughout the woods and surrounding countryside behind our house. The locations are dotted around, seemingly at random, and I have sprinkled seed sparsely and randomly. This makes the growing crops fit in with their surroundings. If I had planted them in the normal way for growing vegetables - with regimented spacing and rows, they would look like a vegetable garden and be eaten. Instead, as my plots are random and look like they are part of the local environment, they're left alone. Most people can't identify food, whether it's growing wild or not. In experiments with friends when I walked them past some of my wild plots, nobody was able to identify growing carrots or cabbages.

It's good to get a supply of seeds that will provide you with food all the year round. You should have enough packets so that you can take some with you to a new location if you have to escape. Keep them in your bug out bag.

Vegetables on their own won't provide you with enough nutrients to live off, so you'll need to supplement your diet with whatever else you can find. You can choose whatever vegetables you like, but remember that you're growing survival food - you shouldn't be silly and exclude certain vegetables just because you don't like them.

You should also read up about vegetable growing and how to protect them from pests and diseases, how and when to sow and harvest them, how to store and preserve etc.

Here are the varieties that I have in my bug out bag -

Broccoli
Carrot
Courgette
Leek
Lettuce
Onion
Spinach
Tomato
Turnip

I hate turnips, they're absolutely disgusting, but I've chosen all these because they're very easy to grow and they have long harvest periods. Spinach in particular, can be harvested all year round. Courgettes grow prolifically and they can be dried and stored easily.

Seed packets should have the sowing and harvesting dates printed on them, but you can extend the harvest period by sowing the seeds at two week intervals.

Here's a tip for you - don't buy organic seed. Non-organic seed is usually coated with a harmless treatment which stops the seed rotting once it's in the soil. Organic seed doesn't have this coating, meaning the seed can be harder to germinate.

In normal conditions there's usually no problem at all getting organic seeds to germinate, but we don't know what stress conditions nature will be under at the end of the world, do we? Best to give the seeds a bit of a helping hand.

Once your vegetables have grown, you can take seeds from them to use again! You can see the seeds in tomatoes, so you just need to remove them and let them dry out, then they'll be

ready to use next year. Some vegetables will need to be left to grow beyond their harvest period, to let them "go to seed". This basically means the plant is past its best - you can't eat it, but it has produced seed heads for you.
The usual way to spot that a vegetable has gone to seed is that the vegetable starts wilting and changing colour, and it then produces a flower head which contains the seeds.
The process for each vegetable is different, so it's best to learn all this now while you've still got time.
Here's another tip - don't buy F1 hybrids. You'll spot these because after the name of a vegetable it will have "F1", eg Tomato Shirley F1.
This means that the variety has been created by breeding two different varieties. If you saved the seeds from these varieties then whatever grows from them could be inedible. They might not be inedible, but you just won't be able to tell until it's too late.

Bugging Out

As I said earlier, a bug out bag contains only what you need to survive a relocation. Of course, you don't know how long that relocation will take, so you have to be able to carry enough to keep you going for a few days. It's a tricky balancing act because you shouldn't be carrying absolutely everything with you, but you also want to give yourself the best possible chance of survival and of setting up somewhere new.
You'll need to carry enough so that you've got the best chance, but also you'll need the bag to be light enough to allow you to run and fight.

I see the bug out bag as being a temporary survival kit only, because your goal should always be to create a defensible position from where you can go out scavenging etc, and to where you can return in safety to your family.

You'll read lots of different advice on what you should put in your bug out bag, but the reality is that aside from some

common sense essentials, you're likely to have a personal preference for what you think is vital equipment.
There are some undeniable essentials which you need to make sure you've got covered, and they are -

Food
Weapons
Warmth
First Aid
Shelter

I'm a firm believer in travelling light on the basis that if you stuff your bug out bag with everything then it may be too heavy to run and fight with, and if you lose it then you've lost everything. Personally, I like to have the bare essentials in my bug out bag, but I also have a secure stash of supplies and equipment than I can retrieve once I've relocated.

I have a 40 litre rucksack that I use as a bug out bag. It goes without saying that a rucksack is the best idea, as it leaves your hands free while you're wearing it.
In that rucksack I have -

Knife Sharpener
Vegetable Seeds
Lightweight Tarpaulin
First Aid Kit
Toothbrush
12 Inch Crowbar
Knife
Survival Food
Paracord
Collapsible Water Bottle
Water Filter
Solid Fuel Stove
Mess Tins (for cooking in and eating out of)
Spare Underwear
Lightweight Rain Coat
Firestarter

Hand Sanitiser
Loo Roll
Trowel
Torch
Wind Up Radio
Multi Vitamins

I also have a bug out belt with pouches that contain -

Snares
Fishing Kit
Water Filter
Water Bottle
Multi Tool
Knife Sharpener
Compass
Torch
First Aid Kit
Firestarter
Small Binoculars
Lifeboat Biscuits

On top of this, I would expect to have either a knife and backup on my belt, or a knife and machete.

It has been suggested to me by a friend that my bug out bag has too few things in it, but as I said earlier, there's a lot of personal preference at work when you choose the contents of your bag.
I lived for a while owning nothing except a tin opener and the clothes I was wearing, so I know that it is possible to survive on much less than you'd imagine. In fact I look at my bug out bag contents and I think it's very luxurious!
I have also been told that I have too much in my bug out bag, which I disagree with entirely. It is very light and it allows me to set up from scratch and build up a base of comfort. Saying that, there's no real need to have a solid fuel stove, but I like to keep it because then all of my family will be able to cook. They can't all make a wild fire (two of them are very young).

But again, it's personal preference and your own bag may look very different. Some people only put food in their bag, or weapons, and that's just daft.

So, you've got your bug out bag on your back, a couple of knives on your belt (maybe a machete too), and you're on your way to your bug out location.

How long can you survive on the journey?
How about when you get to your location - how long can you survive there?

As you journey to your next safe location, you are not simply enjoying a leisurely stroll with your family. You should all be aware of potential dangers, and you should all know which plants to be looking out for as you go.
Even in winter there is plenty of wild food available, although not all of it is nutritious enough to allow you to survive on it alone. You'll have to supplement the wild food with more substantial things, and in a survival situation you can't be picky.
I like pizza but there won't be any at the end of the world. Instead I'll have to eat moss, which is bitter and horrible (never eat yellow moss as it is poisonous).

In a real world, end of the world survival situation, perhaps a more relevant question than "how long can you survive" is "how long are you prepared to survive?"
That's why mental fortitude is possibly the most important asset any survivor can have. When the shit hits the fan, are you prepared to sleep in a bush somewhere, never really sleeping for fear someone is going to kill you? Are you prepared to eat bugs, kill livestock for food, or steal food off someone else?
I'm hoping you'll have remembered the "Training" part of the three keys to survival, and you'll have studied how to get food from nature, which plants are safe to eat, how to fish and snare etc, then you won't need to take food from other survivors.

Common sense tells us people will fight each other over food. You might not do it yourself, but survivors will kill survivors over food. It's happened in every country on the planet when there's been starvation. People get beaten up, crushed, stampeded etc during New Year sales, so imagine the carnage when it's not a posh TV that people want, but their very survival.

I've read that in the very worst cases of mass starvation cannibalism takes hold, and although we all think we would never be cannibals, the human desire for survival is stronger sometimes than the natural constraints which tell us certain behaviour is wrong. During the siege of Leningrad there was apparently widespread cannibalism, although if a cannibal was caught they were summarily executed.
I haven't been able to find any modern day examples of famine induced cannibalism, but I firmly believe it would happen in a long term survival situation.

I have lifeboat biscuits in my bug out belt. They taste of rock hard cardboard but they have enough calories to keep you going. It is never going to be good enough to prepare for the end by buying up a year's supply of MREs or freeze dried food. It could be taken off you or contaminated somehow, and if you have to leave your home and travel a great distance, how are you going to carry it?
Of course it is sensible to stock up on a healthy supply of this stuff, as it lasts for ages and will keep hunger at bay.
It isn't cheap though, and we're not all rich.
You can get recipes to make your own lifeboat biscuits online. That's what I do, and it means you can mess around with the ingredients to try and make the things more tasty.

But being able to identify wild plant food and to butcher wild game is far more important than having a good stash of commercially prepared survival food.
It means you can travel light, harvesting food as you go. The majority of people won't know what's safe to eat, so there

should be plenty for you. And don't forget to raid the local allotments too.

Bugging Out Where?

When you are planning for your eventual bug out, it makes sense to have at least a couple of different scenarios in mind. I've already mentioned that you should have several alternative plans for while you are actually on the move, for example if your primary location has been compromised where is your backup, and if that one is also no good, where are you going then? We need to plan like this so that we're never left in the open not knowing what to do. If we're on our own then we're able to react and change depending on the situation, but if we have our family in tow then it's vital that everyone knows what's going on in any given situation, so that if you're all separated you each know how to meet up again.

But in terms of making a plan for the bug out, I would suggest two scenarios to think about.
The first is to make a plan for a rapid, potentially violent emergency escape, such as you might find in a total shit hits the fan situation.
The second is to plan for a more gradual departure, as might be necessary if your local situation worsens over time. You could, for example, find your area at risk of contamination or under threat of attack, the focus point for refugees etc.

In this book we're really thinking more along the lines of an absolute shitstorm, rather than a gradual breakdown of society, but even after the storm there'll be periods of relative calm and adjustment. Any such period will come in ebbs and flows though, so you'll have to be prepared for a decline in your situation and plan accordingly.

So for example, as soon as the shit hits the fan I will barricade my house as best I can using the materials I have already prepared and got ready. I will be attaching barriers to the doors and windows, sealing the internal doors, booby trapping the carpet with nails, and taking up the stairs. My family and I will live upstairs.

There's clearly a fair amount of work to be done to secure the house in this way, but obviously I'd plan to do it immediately rather than wait to be attacked.

Then if we needed to make a rapid escape we would get up into the attic and break out through the roof tiles. We will then be able to get into neighbouring houses via their roof tiles or loft windows (we're in a terrace).

My plan under the second situation - the slow build up to departure - depends on a variety of local factors, and by necessity the plan has to be more fluid.
I could, for example, head to my place of work with its spiked 7ft fence all around, it's armoured windows and its steel shuttered doors. But that's 40 miles from my house along the M25, which is notoriously packed even on a quiet day. I could of course travel cross country, but I'd have my young family with me and 40 miles is plenty of distance in which something could go wrong.

If I'm planning on permanently leaving my home and making my office my primary defensible position, I might want to take my supplies with me which means I'd need a car. Personally I wouldn't trust the roads to be clear over 40 miles.
In truth it's hard to prepare for a gradual departure because there will be factors which you may not be aware of, despite your best efforts. Communication will be sparse, you're very unlikely to be able to use a phone, so the only way you'll be able to tell whether a planned destination is safe, is to go there yourself and recce it.
I currently have three different locations in mind for if I had time to plan and recce a relocation.

In truth, even a slow build up can change to chaos in a matter of seconds. When a situation changes it often happens very quickly after a slow and ominous build-up. It's like an elastic

band stretching and stretching until the point when it snaps. In a survival situation the build up, or the stretching, will be the realisation that we're in trouble. People will initially mill around watching the situation and each other.
The snap will be the point when the first person decides to act. They'll do what everyone else was thinking of doing (such as looting a shop or kicking in a neighbour's door), and that will be the catalyst for everyone else joining in.

EDC - Every Day Carry

One of the pouches on my bug out belt contains my EDC kit. This is a very small collection of things that will help in an emergency if I am away from home.
I take the pouch off the belt and take it with me when I drive any distance, and when I'm at work.
The law about carrying knives in the UK means that you can only have an unlockable knife with a blade of less than three inches. Personally I don't think the risk is worth it, so I don't have one. Although it's legal to carry one, I don't fancy trying to explain why I have it if I'm stopped.
My EDC kit contains a Lifestraw water filter and some liferaft biscuits, together with a poncho and some paracord for shelter, a torch and a firestarter, and that's it. Anything else can be obtained while I'm in transit.
Some EDC kits contain a tactical pen, which is a kubotan in disguise. Although it is an effective weapon, the Police are aware of them and you'll have to explain yourself if your stopped. Remember that if the shit has hit the fan while you're in transit, any remaining law and order is likely to be draconian at least in the early days. There may be martial law or heavy restrictions on movement.
I can think of nothing worse than being stranded many miles away from my family and my supplies, arrested and put in a refugee camp for having a weapon on me. That's a worst case scenario obviously, I'm just saying that in an EDC kit a weapon isn't necessarily a good choice.

Self Defence

Have you heard of the "fight or flight" reflex? This is where a person is threatened and their natural response is either to fight back or run away. Each response is better in different circumstances, and the trick is to learn to make a conscious decision about your best course of action, rather than let your reflexes kick in and take control of you.
For example, I never ran, and sometimes I should have. The best defence against a knife is to run, providing you've got enough of a headstart, you're faster than the attacker, and you're not trying to protect anyone. I hated the idea of looking like a coward, so I used to stand and fight even when I wasn't very good at fighting, and I have the scars to prove it. Alternatively, one of my friends used to run at every threat. This meant he'd leave his friends behind to fight alone, and one day he didn't run fast enough and his attacker caught up with him...

What I'm trying to say is that "fight or flight" is natural, but it's not healthy in my opinion. It needs to be trained out of you so that you're better able to protect yourself and your family. This can be done by increasing your self confidence, and for the purposes of self defence, this is achieved by improving your cardiovascular fitness, your strength, and your fighting ability. So go for a run, do some weights, and go to a decent martial arts class. Over the years I have learnt Karate, Wing Chun, Tae Kwon Do, Kickboxing, Krav Maga and Ju Jitsu and I can thoroughly recommend the last two as being the best, based on real life experiences of defending myself. Krav Maga in particular is very easy to learn and in no time at all you'll have the confidence to defend yourself and your family. Ju Jitsu is good because it's all about locks, pressure points and grappling. You don't want a fight to end up on the ground, but if it does then Ju Jitsu will teach you how to win.
Krav Maga was developed by the Israeli military, so it will teach you how to defend yourself against both fist fighters and

armed assailants. It is all about ending a fight quickly, which is exactly what you need.

A real fight is not nice. Close your eyes and imagine being cornered in a ruined building at night, with a baying mob of machete and bat wielding thugs running towards you. How the hell are you going to defend yourself? There's nowhere to run, so what on earth are you going to do?
A fight like that is truly medieval. There is no sparring, it's just whacking and slashing brutality.

Next imagine running for your life until your lungs burn and your legs stop working, but if you stop you'll get stabbed by the gang that's chasing you. Then you see a different gang of people up ahead, ready to cut you off. So you've got knife wielding attackers behind you, knife wielding attackers ahead of you, and you're going to have to fight for your life despite being exhausted... To make it worse, you have your family with you and you must protect them.

I was once attacked by a gang of God knows how many yobs. It felt like there were hundreds of them, but I'm sure it wasn't that many. I have no idea what prompted it but I think they thought I was someone else.
There isn't any way to fight that many people. I was on my own and the best I could do was give two of them a battering before I was mobbed and kicked unconscious. If it had been an end of the world situation and they'd had knives, I wouldn't have had a chance.
That's why when the shit hits, you have to move through your local area as if you were a soldier moving through enemy territory. You can't allow yourself to be taken by surprise. You must be constantly scanning the land ahead on the lookout for people trying to hide themselves, and if you can't see far enough ahead, you don't go in that direction.

Our American cousins will say that if you're surrounded by knife wielding gangs, you should pull out a gun. But we're English and we're not allowed them.

So what do you do when you can't run and you're outnumbered?

The sad truth is that a single survivor, even if he's ex-SAS, would be hard-challenged to fight off a pack of thugs. The American idea of pulling out a gun at a knife fight is the right one though. It's a question of escalation. You have a knife, I have a gun.
I'm not allowed a gun, so you attack me with a knife, I take your eye out.
There has to be enough horror that everyone else pauses and thinks "Bloody hell! I don't want that to happen to me." More disturbingly, there has to be enough ultra-violence to end a fight quickly. You can't be sparring with one attacker while fifty more creep up on you. There's no sparring allowed. You won't have time.
The thing to bear in mind is that your attacker will be in the rush of adrenaline and he may not even feel your punches. You will be under stress so you won't be hitting as accurately or as hard as you could be. Therefore, ultra-violence is the only guaranteed way to end a fight against multiple attackers. This is another area in which Krav Maga excels, because you are taught to fight instinctively rather than analyse every movement and plan your counter attack. Krav Maga will teach you how to end a fight quickly and effectively.

Individual gang members always get in each other's way during a fight, and you may be able to use that to your advantage. Also, it's often the case that the yob who attacks first is the one who needs to prove something to the other gang members. He may be weaker or less experienced than the other members. To counteract this he may actually be more violent than his mates, but there's a good chance he won't be a talented fighter, and he's the one you have to do the ultra-violence on to make everyone else hesitate.
This is where the proactive personality type wins. He's been to martial arts classes and he's a bit tasty, a bit of a geezer, but more importantly, he has self discipline and self confidence. He fights naturally and easily, without having to think about

what move to do, and without having to calm his panicked mind.

Possibly the most important thing to remember in any fight, is to make sure it doesn't end up on the ground. If you wind up on the floor it can end very quickly and very nastily. Even bystanders who have stayed out of a fight may run over and put the boot in.
If you end up fighting for your life on the ground, don't curl up into a ball with your arms over your head, it won't work. Block as many kicks as you can with one arm in a defensive position, and use the other arm to help you to get up as quickly as possible. Getting up has to be your priority over fighting back, particularly if there are multiple assailants.

When you're on the ground your fighting options are limited, unless you've learnt a good ground fighting martial art like Ju Jitsu.
If you have the opportunity, elbow an attacker as hard as you can at the side of their knee, rupturing their knee ligaments. Or you could use a palm heel strike or hammer fist instead of your elbow.
Don't try and aim for their kneecap, just deliver a good powerful blow to the whole side of the knee.
Alternatively, a foot can be grabbed and twisted forcefully inwards (ie towards the other foot), breaking the ankle.

The psychology of fighting means that because we're basically nice people, we might sometimes be worried about hurting the other person. This might sound strange, but believe me, it is true.
We have to condition our minds to turn off this inherent goodness, so we can wallop the other person as hard as we possibly can.

In an end of the world situation, as I have said before, the greatest threat to your life could come from your fellow survivors. In every major disaster both individuals and gangs are quick to take advantage of the situation, and they will be a threat both when you are in your home and when you are travelling.

Gangs can break into your home to steal your supplies. When you're bugging out or simply out looking for food, they can steal your weapons, your boots, your clothes. You have to be prepared.

Gangs will form naturally because the people who are inclined towards violence and cowardice are likely to already be friends. They'll realise that the easiest way to survive is to steal from other survivors, so they'll band together to make it even easier.

Unfortunately, if you try to plan for this eventuality and go out right now to suggest to your neighbours that you all form a protection group in the event of the end of the world, they'll think you are a psycho.

So we'll assume you're on your own and you need to decide on some means to defend yourself.

I've already suggested you go and learn a good martial art. Krav Maga is brilliant but you'll need to find a martial art that you feels right to you.

Finding your martial art is strangely like buying a house or meeting your soulmate - you kind of "know" that this is the one for you. Try to avoid something overly stylistic such as Karate. You want a real world fighting skill. The best classes are the ones with realistic sparring, which might make you feel uncomfortable but it will be worth it.

Lets look at some weapons... All these are currently available to all residents of the UK, although obviously it is illegal to carry them. I have left out the more obvious self defence weapons such as shotguns and hunting rifles, purely because they are not available to everyone.

Sword

A sword has the advantage of having a long reach. This makes it both intimidating and practical as a self defense weapon. A sword could be used purely defensively to force a knife wielding opponent to keep his distance, and offensively it can both stab and slash.

The sword has a weakness though, which tends to make it unreliable and a poor choice as your primary defensive weapon. Remember, you want a weapon that will save your life, not a cheap useless thing that breaks.

Although swords are made from hardened steel, unless you spend several hundred pounds on one it will be a poor quality steel. You are unlikely to be able to tell that just from looking at the sword. A poor quality steel breaks easily and it doesn't hold its edge. This means you'll be constantly sharpening the edge and worrying about it breaking just when you need it most. Bending the blade will break it, as will a machete blow.

Machete

Machetes have gained popularity as a weapon in the UK over recent years. They have always been used effectively overseas, but they've taken a while to be considered a mainstream weapon over here.

The power of a machete lies in its strength. Designed for hacking down jungles, the blades are thick and brutal. They do not have as sharp an edge as a sword, but they can be ground down if you choose. Just remember that a sharp edge generally needs sharpening more often.

Some machetes have been designed with a stabbing point, some have saw edges on the top of the blade. Care need to be taken when choosing a machete, as there are plenty of blades out there that are designed more for aesthetic appeal than practicality.

Knife

Seeing a knife in someone's hand can cause a victim to freeze. There is no greater sign of an aggressor's intent than the sight of a knife. This scumbag means to do you harm.

A knife can be a kitchen knife, a combat knife, or a survival knife. There's not much difference between a survival knife and a combat knife, other than the design of a survival knife is slightly less threatening. Avoid those survival knives with a hollow handle which has been filled with useless survival trinkets. You want a full tang blade where the blade steel goes all the way to the end of the handle.

Everyone has got a different opinion when it comes to knife choices. A good example of a great all-round knife is the Cold Steel GI Tanto, and this is just because it has extreme simplicity of design, and the blade is tough enough to be severely abused in the wild. It will let you chop wood, dig a pit etc without damage, and it looks intimidatory too. I'm not a fan of Kydex sheaths though - again it's just personal preference - I prefer cordura or leather.

Avoid kitchen knives as the blades are too thin. A decent knife will have a thick enough blade that allows you to chop wood. Some survival knives have a firestarter, blade sharpener, compass etc in the sheath. It's best to get these extras separately, because if the ones in the sheath are the only ones you have and you lose the sheath, you're buggered.

Backup Knife
Just in case your main knife is taken off you, breaks or gets lost. A good backup knife should be able to perform some of the same functions as your main knife. Obviously being smaller it won't be as effective at chopping wood, but for everyday camp tasks and for self defence, there are plenty of good choices out there.

Airgun
An air rifle could be used for hunting rabbits and pigeons, and as a self defence weapon nobody would want to be shot by one.
An air rifle uses air to fire either a .22 or .177 calibre pellet, usually using a bolt action arrangement. Modern rifles have a rotary magazine.
Air pistols won't be any good for hunting, but as a self defence weapon they could be effective at very short ranges. They won't drop anyone, but the pellets bloody hurt and require digging out of your skin.

An air pistol is comparatively low powered, but I wouldn't like to be shot by one. They fire .177 pellets via a small CO2 cannister hidden in the grip. More often than not they look like military handguns (Beretta, SIG etc), and they can fire their full magazine of 8 pellets as quickly as you can pull the trigger. They don't have the power to stop someone running at you, but as a visual deterent they're effective.

Crossbow
Crossbows are lethal, so it's very surprising that they are so easily available in the UK. Pistol crossbows use a clever cocking mechanism to draw the string back ready for the next shot. The bolts are lightweight and only effective at very short ranges.
Full stock crossbows are fearsomely powerful. The bolts are still lightweight, but the bow can fire the bolts at around 250 feet per second at a strength of 175lb. That's the same power as a 12 stone person travelling at 170mph.
They are slow to load though, and you'll often need a special winding device to draw the string back. Remember to have plenty of spare parts and lots of bolts.
I wouldn't necessarily classify these as a self defence weapon, if only because they are so slow to make ready for the next shot. As a visual deterent they can only be beaten by a gun, and there's no doubt they would make people think twice about attacking you.

Bow
Not as powerful as a crossbow, but still a potent weapon in the right hands. Modern bows are easy to use and very accurate, although they don't have the same range as a crossbow. They are quicker to load though.

Catapult
Accurate, quick to load, and supremely painful, these are effective at short ranges. They fire steel ball bearings of various sizes.

Spear
I've not seen any for sale ever, so you'll need to make one out of a broom handle with a knife taped on to the end. I imagine these would be quite effective as a self defense weapon, especially in your home with short jabbing thrusts in a narrow hallway.

Axe
Axes are available either as traditional woodsmen versions with long handles and a heavy head, as shorter camp hatchets, and as modern paramilitary style beasts. Go online and look at the Sog Voodoo Hawk for example. The Sog is designed purely for combat and is ineffective at chopping wood long term. Something like the Sog can be thrown at an aggressor, but remember that if you miss they can retrieve it and use it against you.
A small hatchet can be a very versatile tool both in the camp and as a self defence weapon.

Chainsaw
Forget about chainsaws. They'd undoubtedly make effective deterrents to home invasion though, if you stood out the front revving it up.

Hammer
A good example of using whatever comes to hand as an effective weapon, hammers have been used in battles for centuries. You can get a hammer loop for your belt to make it easily accessible. I bet we've all accidentally hit ourselves with a hammer at some point, so we all know how much it hurts.

Baseball Bat or Golf Club
A bat or club is very easy to wield, they cause a huge amount of pain, you don't really need any training to use one, and they are a good visual deterent.
Despite the incredible pain they can administer, they won't always drop an attacker straight away though, if you get them in the wrong place for example.

Bats and clubs can break quite easily.

Torch
These can be used either as a blunt force weapon if they're heavy enough (a big Maglite for example), or as a distraction device.
For less than £20 you can get a 2000 lumen CREE torch (insanely bright), which could be used to dazzle and disorientate an aggressor. They usually have flashing modes too, which blast pulses of violently bright light many times a second. At night time that's the last thing an aggressor would want in their face, and it gives you the opportunity to either run away or incapacitate your aggressor.

Improvised Weapons
Almost anything can be turned into a weapon, it just depends on the thing's construction, your ingenuity, and your skill in wielding it. A pen, for example, makes an effective stabbing weapon when you strike an attacker in the face or head with it. Keys can make a good flail, a can of aerosol spray and cigarette lighter make a flamethrower, and anything sharp or heavy is basically a weapon.

Clothing

This is a tricky balancing act between being comfy and practical, and also being discreet. You don't want to draw attention to yourself and find yourself being targeted by people who want to take what's yours.
I remember when I was growing up in the dodgier areas of London, you couldn't wear certain brands of jeans or trainers because people would mug you for them.
A survival situation is no different. You run the risk of making yourself stand out as a target purely because you are better prepared than most people and your equipment will be better suited to the new, harsher conditions than others.
If you're walking around dressed like Mad Max, openly displaying your military quality clothes and your armour and weapons, then you could be asking for trouble.

Your clothing may differ depending on your current circumstances. For example, while you are in your house quietly watching and listening, consolidating your supplies etc, you may choose to wear your everyday casuals. Obviously you'll never let your guard down entirely, and you'll have a good knife on your belt and your bug out bag ready to grab. Personally, I also have the bug out belt. It's a belt with carry pouches containing the bare minimum of essentials - first aid kit, torch, paracord, lifeboat biscuits, firestarter and a few small tools.
If I were relaxing at home I would be wearing the belt at all times.

If you were still in the early days of worldwide disaster and the times of comparative relaxation had not yet arrived, you might prefer to wear tough, military clothing such as a tactical top, ripstop trousers, combat boots, hard knuckle gloves and elbow and knee pads. Maybe a helmet too, to protect against bats, and a scary balaclava to round off the ensemble. I actually recommend blokes to have a "cup" - one of those hard things you wear in cricket and martial arts to protect your family jewels.

A military looking outfit could either make people think twice about attacking you, or it could make people (particularly gangs) want to take it all off you. Apart from the visibly valuable equipment you're wearing, you could make yourself look like you have possessions at home or in your pockets worth protecting.
Often, being discreet is better than being gung-ho, but only you will be able to make that decision.

I have seen some peoples' end of the world kits which contain what look to be combat helmets, but on closer inspection they turn out to be airsoft helmets. These may protect your noggin from a glancing blow, but it won't protect you from any proper violence.

Neither will cycling or paragliding helmets. Motorcycle helmets are used the world over in riots, both for protection and to conceal identity, but they block some sound and vision and will make you less aware of your surroundings. In a violent situation this could prove fatal. A decent helmet will also make a handy weapon in dire circumstances.

While we're on the subject of protective clothing, it makes good sense to have something to protect your forearms from defensive injuries while you are parrying knives or bats.
You can buy protective pads from martial art supply shops, but you can make pads which are just as good...
You need two large hand towels, the cheaper ones are usually better because they're made of tougher material. You will also need some sticky parcel tape or either strapped velcro or strong elastic.
Fold the towel lengthways, then fold it horizontally in half, then horizontally in half again so you are left with a squarish wad. Then use the parcel tape, the elastic or velcro to fix it to your forearm.
Obviously a direct hit with a baseball bat or hammer is still going to break your arm, and a stab with a good knife will go through it. But you'll be well protected from a slash or a glancing blow, and anyway, this is for added protection during parrying - it's not supposed to make you invincible.
You can be the best martial artist in the world, but when you are under the stress of a real world fight for your life, you'll make mistakes, or slow down, or be inaccurate in your strikes, or your strikes will lack your usual power. A bit of forearm protection could make all the difference.

Only you can decide whether you are prepared to buy every item of clothing you could ever need, to be prepared for whichever way the world will end.
If there's a biblical flood have you got scuba gear?
If there's a nuclear war have you got NBC kit?
etc
Are you getting survival clothes for yourself or for everyone in your family?

Whatever your clothing preference is, you need to choose things that are very tough and very comfortable, because it may need to last for very many years.

A good belt is essential, not only because you're going to lose weight over the coming weeks, but because a belt kit is often more practical and more comfortable than a rucksack. It won't be able to carry anywhere near as much as you'd like though, so it's really for emergencies.

I like to think that if I was walking along wearing my bug out bag (rucksack), and I got jumped and lost the bag, my belt kit would keep me alive.

I've said it before but it is worth saying again. You have to decide for yourself whether it's better to go out dressed for battle, or whether it is better to be discrete. Even if you have a solid awareness of the current situation it's hard to make a sound judgement because violent events are notoriously fluid. I've seen it happen where the better skilled fighter, or the better equipped one, is ganged up on because people either want his stuff or they want to prove they are tougher.

For example, lets say it is night time. Or rather, it's the middle of the day but it is as dark as hell outside. There is no power so the streetlights are out and no light comes from any of the houses in your street. Two days ago the pavements were filled with neighbours anxiously asking each other what was going on, whether anyone had heard any news. There were rumours about a supervolcano exploding and sending so much crap into the atmosphere that we were in a nuclear winter. There were no TV or radio signals, and nobody had a mobile signal. The phone lines didn't work and there was no sign of the government.

Ash had started to fall from the skies, coating the neighbourhood in a kind of doom laden snow. The air smelled of burning and everyone was hoarse from breathing the stuff in.

There is a strange silence in your street, but muffled by the falling ash you can just make out screaming and shouting in

the middle distance, in the direction of the local supermarket. You can see the curtains in your neighbours' houses twitching as people look out.
Just then you see a car moving slowly up the street, its headlights blazing. It stops outside one of the houses and you recognise the driver as someone who lives in your street. You run out and ask if if he's heard any news.
He tells you he went to the supermarket to try and get food, but it's been stripped clean by looters. The shutters have been bashed in by a lorry, and the shelves are bare. Even the stationery aisle has been ransacked. He says he saw people being stabbed. He says the streets in the town are crowded with people breaking into the shops.
That was yesterday.
Today you are woken by the sounds of shouting, screaming and breaking glass. There are hundreds of people in the street outside, running, fighting, breaking into houses. There are out of control fires raging in some of the houses and bodies lying in the street.
You see the bloke who lives opposite carrying his young daughter in his arms as he's bundled out of his own house by strangers. They hit him and shout at him as he goes past, then they disappear inside and steal his food. He can't defend himself, his family or his stuff.
People swarm into the houses. It doesn't take long to kick the front doors in. You see a couple of shotguns, a hunting rifle. Many of the teenage kids from the dodgy estate have got pistol crossbows, knives and bats. There are a couple of axes and various gardening tools like spades and forks.
When someone runs out of a house with food, they're attacked by others. There's no real organisation yet, a few clear groups, but it's more of a free-for-all at the moment. People in the crowds are getting stabbed or beaten by others in the crowd, and there's no obvious reason other than primeval bloodlust. It's a bit like a medieval battlefield outside. You see people being stabbed. You suspect from the screams that within some of the houses there may be some rapes.
Yobs throw petrol bombs into houses as they leave.
This is a fight for survival. Kill or be killed.

The odds are against you because there are no sides. There's nobody to help you. You must stay inside and defend your family, because if you step outside you'll die.
In this situation I would suggest wearing whatever protection you have available, and carrying whichever weapons you feel you need. If this is an all-out battle where people are being killed and there are no sides, just a free for all, a kill or be killed medieval chaos, then anything that gives you an edge could just be the thing that ensures your family's survival.

Here's a different scenario...
You are travelling around your local area. You have a safe place to go back to, and you are out looking for food and gathering info about the surrounding area. You are talking to fellow survivors too, and trying to get the bigger picture.
Because the situation has worsened over the past few days with food and water becoming more and more scarce, people are generally more desperate and aggressive. Gangs have formed. Some exist purely to steal, kill and rape, and others fancy themselves more as a kind of paramilitary police force. They try to control particular areas under the pretence of defending against looters and killers, but the reality is that they will take whatever they want from the people they stop.
The roads are jammed with abandoned vehicles, and crowds of angry refugees slow your progress. People carry what they can of their possessions, and many are regularly beaten up or stabbed as food or water is wrestled from their grasp.
A man with a shotgun is set upon by a large group, with each person desperate to get his weapon. It is eventually seized by a woman after its owner is stabbed by several different people, but then she in turn is stabbed many times and the shotgun changes hands again.
In the distance you see an organised gang armed with shotguns, hunting rifles and crossbows. They have organised themselves into a thieving unit, and they are confiscating anything they like the look of. Anyone who resists is savagely beaten with rifle butts.
Assuming the situation is extremely tense but there is no immediate threat to you, you are often better off trying to fit in

with the crowd and being anonymous. I would even leave my bug out belt behind, and instead just have a folded up bag in one of my trouser pockets for whatever wild food I find. Because you are not dressed like Mad Max, dripping with weapons, armour, and a rucksack full of supplies, you don't stand out as someone who has anything worth taking.
Of course, the reality of the situation is that you will have armed yourself discreetly. You will always be able to defend yourself at a moment's notice.

Equipment

Everyone will have a different idea of which equipment is vital, and of course there are different brands and prices. The key thing is obviously that whatever piece of kit you choose should be reliable and last for as long as possible. You are, after all, trusting your life to it.
Some survival gear is expensive but either poorly made or impractical in a real world situation, and other kit is cheap and poorly made. It's a minefield out there!
Another thing to bear in mind is that some kit is designed for short term use to get you out of trouble, and it won't last forever. I'm thinking in particular of some of the fishing kits you can get.
This list is by no means a recommendation, I'm just listing the various things that most of us agree are vital. I haven't included the items which I personally think are pointless, such as generators. Generators don't fit in with my view that we need to to be discreet. We shouldn't be advertising our success with noisy generators.

Water Filter
This is one of the most important pieces of equipment you will own, and you should have several. Every member of my family has several of their own filters.
I keep one in my bug out bag, one in my bug out belt, one in my home stash and then I have a couple more in different caches.

We can only survive for three days without water, and drinking contaminated water could kill you. There are some things you can do to mitigate problems if you don't have a filter, such as taking water from as far upstream as possible, boiling it, using sand, pebbles etc to filter it, or maybe you have purification tablets.

There are many different types of filter on the market. My personal preference is for one that's like a straw. It will clean 1500lt of water before it needs replacing.

You can dip one end in a stream and suck water through the device, or you can fill a water bottle or bag and suck through it, or you can squirt the bottle of water through the straw into another container.

I like this one because I like to travel light. It's a throwback to my homeless days. With the straw I can carry a water bottle on my belt and resupply whenever I need to, or I can use the same filter to provide water for my family.

In my home stash and caches I have bottled water, but assuming I have to bug out, I won't be taking the water with me because it is too heavy and cumbersome. A litre of water weighs something like 1kg, so it quickly adds up when you try to take it all with you.

Multi Tool

A good multi tool will include pliers, wire cutters, a saw and a blade as an absolute minimum, but most of them have got several other utility tools too.

Personally I like the multi tools manufactured by Gerber, but there are other good brands. Stanley come a close second. The weak point on multi tools is the wire cutters. If the manufacturer has used cheap steel then the cutters take a dent rather than cut through the wire. Wire cutters are important in your survival gear because you may need to cut through chain link fencing. They won't cut through anything stronger though, like handcuff chains or padlocks.

Main Knife

I divide knives into three categories - a main knife, a backup knife, and a camp knife.

A main knife is one that is equally effective at chopping wood and at self defence. For the purposes of self defence a knife just has to look intimidating.

Knives are another area where everyone has a personal preference, and you are unlikely to ever find total agreement amongst survivors, as to which knife is best.

Schrade make various models which fit the bill nicely, although I have read reports by some users who say they've managed to break the tip off their knives.

The Cold Steel GI Tanto is a fine dual purpose knife. It looks terrifying and as it has such a thick blade it is perfect for chopping wood and general campground abuse. It has a very simple construction too, which is always a bonus.

First Aid

You should make up your own first aid kit because the pre-packed ones are unlikely to include the things you will need in a survival situation.

Obviously plasters, slings and bandages, antiseptic, tweezers, eye patches. The most important thing is to get some training in first aid, because when the shit hits it will no longer be first aid, it will be ONLY aid. Lots of people forget about tweezers. Apart from removing splinters, a good set of needle nose grips will be necessary for pulling out airgun pellets if you've been unlucky enough to be shot.

Watch

I mentioned watches earlier as an example of how you can waste your money.

I have a kinetic watch made by Pulsar. It has kept perfect time for years, is waterproof, and as it is an analogue watch rather than digital, I can use it as a compass.

(Hold the watch horizontally and point the hour hand at the sun. Half way between the hour hand and the 12 o'clock position is south).

Admittedly my watch doesn't look as macho as the toughened digital watches designed for the outdoors, but I am more interested in ability than appearance. During the times I've been chopping wood in the camp or even during martial arts training, I haven't found myself worrying about my watch getting damaged, despite its lack of armour.

Wire Saw

Not really essential if you have a machete or hatchet, but useful to have because they take up minimal room.

These are toughened wire things with a grip on each end and cutting teeth all along. They are great for sawing through small branches and bones.

Torch

I have a solar powered torch and a few battery powered ones, and of course, a supply of spare batteries. One of the torches is a powerful CREE 2000 lumen beast, which is in my self defence stash because of its ability to dazzle and disorientate an attacker.

We have several small torches rather than a big maglite or a camp lantern, on the basis that smaller torches are far easier to carry and take up less room.

Firestarter

Fire is good for morale as well as cooking. We have a couple of Clipper lighters and most of us in the family can make fire with a ferrocerium rod and steel (not the youngsters). I know some people like to have Zippos in their kit, but I've found the fuel evaporates too quickly.

For ferrocerium fire starters I personally like those supplied by The Friendly Swede as the quality is far superior to other brands. Quality can be measured by how quickly you can start a fire. Some brands just give you a few weak sparks but the better quality ones give you a huge shower of them.

Rucksack

This is another area in which you can spend a fortune, and unfortunately it is also an area in which the quality is extremely variable. You don't want to be bugging out with your valuable supplies, only to have things fall out because the stitching has come apart.

I have a SUNVP 40lt rucksack which I have had for years. I wouldn't go any bigger than 40lt because then it might get too heavy to carry, bearing in mind you might be running and fighting while wearing it.

Tarpaulin
A tarpaulin with eyelets along the edges is very versatile. It is perfect for rapid shelter building, and it shouldn't cost any more than about £20

Belt Kit
A belt kit should be light enough and small enough that you can wear it continuously without getting annoyed. It should contain the absolute essentials to keep you alive if you lose your bug out bag.
I have a 2 inch belt (with a steel clasp, not a plastic one which could break), and I have threaded on to it several pouches and a water bottle holder.
The pouches contain first aid essentials, a multi tool, torch, water filter, and a couple of other things that will help me survive until I can re-establish myself.

Paracord
A definite essential!
Paracord has a breaking strength of 550lbs, making it extremely versatile. I have only ever used it to make a shelter with my tarpaulin, but it could be used as fishing line, shoe laces, or to tie a door shut, hang equipment from etc.

Backup Knife
A backup knife should be able to do some of the tasks your main knife can do, although as it is likely to be smaller it won't be able to do them all. It's a useful thing to have in case your main knife is broken or taken off you. Mine is made by Schrade.

Camp Knife
I call it a camp knife but usually people call it a lock knife. This is a sturdy knife with a good grip, and razor sharp edge, for

field dressing wild meat and fish. Mine is made by Buck and I have had it for many years.

Solar Powered / Wind Up Radio
Assuming the powers that be have had time to get to their nice, safe, well stocked bunkers in which to play out the end of the world, we can hope for some news from time to time. You don't want to be carrying a supply of batteries if you can help it, so a wind up or solar radio is best.

Pills / Hygiene
These are essential, because in a survival situation a dose of diarrhea could easily kill you. Once you start eating wild foods more frequently than the commercially available stuff you have been used to, you can expect some form of stomach upset even if it is only brief. There are wild foods that help with diarrhea, headaches etc, and you should be studying your SAS Survival Handbook so you can easily identify them.
Pills should include aspirin (good for gargling if you have a sore throat), paracetamol (headaches etc), diarrhea tablets, and any medication you have been prescribed, along with any personal hygiene items you need (like sanitary towels).
I have a couple of small bottles of hand sanitizer - the sort they have in hospitals. It is very concentrated so a little goes a long way.
And don't forget your toothbrush!

Walkie Talkies
Not essential, but good for peace of mind. My family plan is to always stay in close enough contact with each other that communication won't be a problem, but we have a couple of walkie talkies in case we get separated during our bug out.

Candles
You can get tea lights which last for eight hours, and you can buy them in bulk for pennies. Light will help boost morale, but remember that you'll want to stay invisible. Make sure the light can't be seen by hungry marauders.

Poncho

A good poncho has eyelets so that it can be used to create shelter, like the tarpaulin. You can't beat them for rain protection, but the material can be quite noisy so you won't be sneaking up on anyone. I find them a bit annoying because they can restrict your movement, but they are a useful thing to have.

Knife Sharpener

Another essential piece of equipment. I have several.
A course stone is good for putting a fearsome edge on larger tools / weapons such as an axe, machete or billhook. A fine steel is good for honing the edge on smaller knives.
If you have chosen a knife made from a good steel, you won't need to keep sharpening your blades.

Boots

I foresee a time when people could be attacked for their footwear. Tough boots are vitally important because you may be spending most of your time on your feet. They'll be subjected to all sorts of abuse, so you'll need to spend a bit extra and get the best boots you can afford.
My own boots are made by Magnum, and they have lasted eight years so far. During that time I have worn them daily and have given them all sorts of rough treatment including hang gliding, daily three mile runs, long distance walking and martial art training.
I also have some Hi Tec walking boots and they are holding up well.

Folding Saw

Not essential, although they are tougher than the wire saw and take up less room than a hatchet. I have one which I bought at a garden centre, but it is not well made. It is plasticky and bends under load.

Hatchet

I have a Fiskars small splitting axe. The blade is thinner and sharper than a "regular" axe, meaning that it slices through

wood like butter. It is about 44cm long, making it an ideal size for bushcraft.
A hatchet makes camp life much easier, and it has the added benefit of making a useful weapon if necessary.

Books
Do you remember that training is one of the three key principles behind survival?
Nothing can beat actual real world practice, but to put your skills into practice you are going to have to get some theoretical knowledge.
There are lots of good books out there, the main one (which I consider essential) is the SAS Survival Handbook. It is a large book, so I also have the Collins' Food For Free pocket book. I also have a couple of US Army Field Medicine books, which deal with everything including stab wounds, dislocations, breaks, diseases, childbirth etc.
I have been lucky enough to receive comprehensive first aid training in my work, but commercially available courses will never cover everything you need to know for a survival situation. Your best bet is to find a survival medicine course.

Bow
I would personally suggest forgetting about a long bow, as you will not be accurate enough to use it for hunting without lots of practice.
A crossbow, on the other hand, can be used both defensively and to hunt for food. Make sure to have plenty of spare strings and arrows.

Snares
You must learn how to use a snare properly, because in unskilled hands they can cause untold suffering. A vital part of your kit once you've learned to use them.

Fishing Kit
You can get ready made survival fishing kits which contain all you need to catch your dinner in a survival situation. BCB

make a couple of these kits, or you could look up what's in them and then put your own together.

I have caught several fish using one of the BCB ones with a worm lure.

I've seen a few bug out bags which contain the Yo Yo automatic fishing machine. Using this gadget, you extend your line into the river and when a fish grabs the hook, the machine senses the tension and automatically winds the fish in. I haven't tried one of these but they have good reviews.

I have mixed opinions personally. I can see that it makes sense to have something fishing for you in the background while you are busy setting up camp, but at the same time, I would expect in a survival situation that rivers and lakes are likely to be popular with other survivors. I don't think I'd want to leave the thing unattended, just because it could get nicked, or the fish it catches could get nicked.

I certainly wouldn't camp near a food and water source in a shit hits the fan situation, because it would be crowded with potentially violent other survivors. My personal preference would be to camp well away from such a place, and to stop off just long enough to catch a fish using one of the more old fashioned kits.

Binoculars

A small pair of binoculars is vital. They allow you to scan the land ahead of your planned path, checking for dangers or supplies. I wouldn't be without mine.

Airgun

Good for hunting small game like rabbits and pigeons, and fairly effective for self defence if only for the visual deterent value. I personally don't own one, if only because it is something extra to carry and I feel I can rely on snares and catapult.

Catapult

I like the Black Widow catapult, purely because I have had it many years. It has had to have a couple of new bands in that time, but it is accurate (with practice) and takes up very little room. Good for hunting and for self defence.

Crowbar
I have a twelve inch crowbar. They are useful pieces of equipment because they can break things up, they can allow you access to places, and they can be used as a weapon. The downside is that they are quite heavy.

Entrenching Tool
Lots of people swear by these. They are folding spades made of steel, often with a fold out pick head and a saw blade. Personally I have never felt the need for one, so I have small but tough trowel in my bug out bag instead.

Mess Tins
For cooking in and eating out of. You don't have to spend much money on these and it doesn't matter if they get bashed and dented.

Compass
For rough navigation you'll need a compass, for anything more detailed you'll need a map. If you have made a comprehensive relocation or bug out plan, you may need a map to get there.
Remember when you're travelling, that gangs and armed individuals will be on the roads too, either relocating themselves or attacking and robbing their fellow survivors. Use the map as a guide only, and try to stick to off-piste travel (ie don't travel on the roads, use the countryside instead).

Conclusion - Are You Prepared?

Let's just consider timescales, because once we realise what we're up against we can get a more honest idea of how prepared we are currently, and what we still need to do to give our families the best possible chance of survival.

We can keep the timescale quite simple -

1. The shit hits the fan
2. Shops are broken into and stripped empty
3. Houses are broken into and stripped empty
4. Casual murder and rape, a medieval existence of ultra-violence and scavenging

Of course we all hope that society will recover, but we can't possibly know when that might be. And I don't want you to think that I am advising a Mad Max style existence where you perpetually treat your fellow survivors as a threat.
There will be groups of survivors who form for mutual help and protection. Groups of decent people like you.

But to be ready for the darker moments of the end of the world you must -

1. Increase your fitness so you can run and fight and run and fight and run and fight.

2. Learn an effective martial art, but more importantly learn when NOT to fight.

3. Learn first aid, remembering that your medical skills will be the ONLY medical help anyone will get in the future. There'll be no ambulances or hospitals.

4. Learn bushcraft. Spend as much time in your local area as possible, identifying edible and medicinal plants. Go wild camping so you can practice fire lighting and living under a tarpaulin while eating wild food.

5. Choose vegetable seeds and identify locations around your home, in your locality and at your bug out location, where you can sow unobtrusively. Learn about storing and seed saving.

6. Stock up on tinned foods with long usage dates, white grain rice, multi vitamins etc. Very basically, look at the calories

on the food your buying. You can survive on less than you think but you need to avoid starving yourself. You'll quickly realise that to maintain a 2500 calorie a day intake (if you're a bloke) will take an awful lot of food. When the end comes you should be supplementing your stored commercial food with wild food, and you should be scavenging amongst empty shops and houses constantly searching for food. You should be sowing seeds too.

7. Stock up on equipment, including weapons. Don't get carried away with having all the trendiest gear. Be sure to read buyer reviews of kit and make sure you choose things which will last.

8. Make a plan to barricade and defend your house, and buy the necessary tools and equipment.

9. Conceal your stashes of food, water and equipment.

10. Have an exit plan and several backup plans too, and make sure everyone in your group knows what the plans are, when each plan comes into play, and what their responsibilities are.

If I have learnt anything it is to keep things simple and to live with less.
There's no point being bogged down with equipment and having no knowledge. What good is your £1499 tactical outdoorsman's watch when you don't have the ability to identify wild food?
What's the point in loading your bug out bag with 100kg of survival gear and gadgets and finding it too heavy to run or fight?
You really only have to worry about a few key things -

Food / Water
Shelter
Self Defence
Medical

That's it! Anything else is just fluff, and you'll find that you can actually survive on a lot less than you might imagine.

Maybe I'll see you in the future...

All the best...

David

david@endoftheworlduk.com

I'm building a website with resources and blogs, give aways etc but it's taking me a while... Sorry!

NEW TITLES COMING SOON!

Wild Food - Finding, Catching, And Scavenging At The End Of The World

Survival Combat - Fighting When Your Life Is On The Line

Survival Bushcraft - Simple Survival For The Unprepared Survivor

Urban Bushcraft - How To Survive The Apocalypse With Minimal Preparation

Printed in Poland
by Amazon Fulfillment
Poland Sp. z o.o., Wrocław